WORKING TO RECOVERY

VICTIM TO VICTOR III

A guide to mental wellness

BY

Ron Coleman, Paul Baker & Karen Taylor

A personal planning tool

Dedicated to Sharon Lefevre

She lives forever

First published by Handsell Publishing 2000
This Edition Published by P&P Press 2003
Printed by Urban Print Dundee Tel: 01382 200864

I.S.B.N. No. 0-9548103-2-5

"If you are looking for answers, don't ask the learned man ask the experienced man". (Chinese Proverb)

PREFACE

This highly original book is inspired by the experience of Ron Coleman, who spent thirteen years in and out of the psychiatric system and who was diagnosed as having a serious mental health problem. In this book Ron collaborates with Karen Taylor (RMN) and Paul Baker (community development consultant) in considering how in spite of all the odds seeming to be stacked up against him, he still managed to make a full recovery.

By a full recovery, we mean that Ron, who had for many years experienced severe emotional distress - which prevented him from working and even sometimes from functioning at all -, managed to pick up his life again. This was a process that was to transform Ron's' life, from being a "victim", constantly hospitalised, heavily medicated, living a life that was fragmented by the disruption his illness caused him - he became "victor". He found a way of harnessing the people around him, to such a constructive effect, that from the point of making the decision that he wanted to recover to the point where Ron could say he was recovered took a surprisingly short period of time.

Ultimately, Ron completely gave up his psychiatric status; this is something that is now in the past. This was by no means an easy journey but it was a worthwhile one. Now, Ron does not regard himself as having a mental illness, he no longer takes medication or receives any other form of treatment. Although Ron still hears voices he does not regard these as a problem and has found his own ways of coping with the other "symptoms" that led him to seek assistance in the first place. What this experience did leave though, was a scar that needed to heal, the recognition that perhaps the thirteen years in and out of psychiatric care need not have happened at all!

As someone who had the privilege to be part of Ron' s life at this time, the two things that struck me about this whole experience were; firstly, after making the decision that he was going to work toward recovery, Ron refused to give in to his illness. Secondly he always asked those people around him to be part of the process of his recovery. In a way we all recovered together, this is not only Ron' s success story, Ron's journey also restored the confidence and self belief of the workers and friends who took part in his recovery. He asked for our best and he gave us his. What I've taken from this is that recovery in many ways is both an individual and collective experience.

When this recovery occurred it seemed to be such an unusual event that professional mental health workers and fellow users of mental health services did not know how to react. They were frankly, suspicious and doubting, either believing that he was wrongly diagnosed or would soon become ill again. To recover from your illness, became for some people rather a threatening development. At the very least the recovery was considered atypical and something that was just one of those things that happen - inexplicable perhaps, but not anything that could be learned from. Ron was strongly affected both by the loss of thirteen years of his life as well as the by the ambivalent response to his recovery. So, over the last eight years he has given much thought to what it was that really happened to enable his recovery.

In this book, the third in a series of workbooks for recovery we look at the lessons that we have been about the recovery process. We have turned these into a practical guide, so that any one who wants to take this journey can benefit from Ron' s experience and the many other people we have talked to about their own recoveries. This book is not intended to be the answer; it is instead a tool for your own recovery journey.

Paul Baker March 2000

Contents

INTRODUCTION
What were the origins of this workbook?

This is the third book in a series of books on recovery, the first looked at hearing voices and the second at self-harm. We saw that the voice experience and self-harm were like a form of intermediate language through which personal distress was being expressed. We believe this is the case with other forms of mental health problems.

The idea behind the workbooks is to offer another way of thinking, other than that, that is current today, which focuses mainly on illness and pathology and often translates for users of services as a message of no future, despair, hopelessness, apathy and fear.

There is a need for another kind of language. A more positive and enabling language that acknowledges the potential of recovery, respects the desire to stop being a victim and to become a victor of your experience and doesn't stand in your way when you seek to find your routes to recovery.

A glossary of terms used in this workbook

Some of the terms we use in the workbook may not always be familiar to you, therefore we have given a brief explanation of what we mean when we use them.

ACTION PLAN

This is fairly self explanatory, we mean the establishment of a plan for your recovery that indicates the action points that you and the professional you are working with have identified and agreed to act on. This could include a timetable for when these activities will take place. For instance your action plan might include regaining employment and as part of your action plan there would be a process identified as to how that would happen (including retraining and gaining new skills; interview techniques; voluntary work placement etc.)

ASSESSMENT

Assessment is an increasingly important procedure used by health and social service authorities to determine the needs of an individual requesting or requiring support. It can also be used as a gate keeping exercise to decide who gets a service and who doesn't. These decisions are based on a list of priorities associated with issues like needs, risk and vulnerability. An assessment though, can also be your opportunity to say what you regard your requirements to be and to have those stated, even if they are not always responded to.

CARE

This term is used a lot in health service language, for instance we have now specific programmes and approaches which seek to ensure that the care received is of the right kind and the right amount. In the section on "My mental health career" we ask about your own experience of procedures known as CARE PROGRAMME/ CARE MANAGEMENT APPROACH and whether you feel that it has been useful to you. We have also some concerns about the use of care in this context, because it seems to be a rather limiting framework, of course "care" is important, but what about personal development issues, are they always covered by this term? Sometimes, but not always, we would prefer the term ACTION PLANNING or RECOVERY PROGRAMME because these words are more explicitly dynamic and more descriptive of a process that involves moving forward.

COPING STRATEGY

A coping strategy is another way of saying how we all try to find a way, or different ways to deal with a problem in our life. It is the way we respond to difficulties, with mental health problems this could mean that overwhelming sadness and anxiety is in itself a way the "self" is trying to make sense of an extremely difficult episode in your life. Although it may seem entirely negative, within this experience is also a positive acknowledgement that there is something that needs to be resolved. For people who hear voices for instance the voice that is saying negative things to you could be regarded as positive because it is drawing attention to an issue in your life that needs to be sorted out.

ENABLING and FACILITATING

Two words with important connections. Both are increasingly used to describe a different kind of involvement by services in the lives of people with mental health problems. Rather than caring for people and intervening only when they are in crisis, with the client being seen mostly as receiving a service determined by the professionals, the terms ENABLING and FACILITATING show a commitment to working alongside the client in resolving their problems. This main difference is between the philosophies of doing things FOR you and doing things WITH you.

EMPOWERMENT
A difficult and often misunderstood term, many people think that is possible to give someone else power. We think that it is the other way round - you must take back the power that has been taken from you - to live your own life, means to be in control of the decisions that you take. We are all involved in power games of differing kinds and throughout our life it remains an important issue (as parents or children; gas workers or managers: as professionals and clients). We regard empowerment as a process of reacquisition and return, this is something that can be facilitated or enabled but not given. For instance, by people not obstructing you in your journey to self-empowerment and by accepting that in recovery it is the recovering person who must lead and the workers who must follow

EXPLANATORY FRAMEWORK
This is a term that we do not hear being used very much; to put it simply it is a person's own belief about what is happening to them. Many psychiatrists believe that mental illness is a biological condition; whilst many users believe that mental distress is caused by life events. We believe that both these explanations should hold equal value.

EXPERTS OF EXPERIENCE
It is not said enough, so we must say it again, you are the expert of your own experience. This expertise has a value, for within your experience lies the possibility of resolution and recovery. It is the unlocking of this expertise that can begin the journey to recovery. This is a message for professionals too, if you recognise this expertise and respect the mutuality of the expertise of experience as being as valuable as your own expertise by profession then you can really be an enabler in the process of recovery.

EXPERTS BY PROFESSION
Because the work book can be a useful tool in developing working relationships between the expert of experience and the expert by profession, it is important you know what it is the professionals have to offer you, what are their skills and background, how do they justify their involvement in your life. Conversely, if you are a professional then it is important to be explicit about your skills, interests and experience and why you think you have something to offer in your relationship with the expert of experience.

INTERMEDIATE LANGUAGE
Actions can sometimes be likened to a language. With mental health problems it is the 'symptoms' or behaviors and experiences that can be thought of as a language. The language is intermediate because it takes the place of vocalising your problems and because of this sometimes has to be decoded to be understood. The code though, is within you.

MAINTENANCE
In the face of increasing demands on services many people are resigned to the fact that it is only possible to provide maintenance support and care to people with mental health problems and to do more is impossible within the current resource constraints. Whilst we agree there is a need to increase the amount of funding and workers, we still believe that current service interventions have the potential for greater effectiveness. This could be achieved by considering how we could do more to support people in their recovery. This should be the number one objective of all services.

MAPPING
Map makers; create the tools that we use to explore our experience. An example of a map would be the personal recovery plan at the end of this book or your care plan. Think of the mapmakers you identify with, this could be a therapist, your key worker or a writer who is assisting you in shaping your thinking.

MENTAL DISTRESS
We prefer this term to other ones commonly used in mental health. This is because it places the stress on the significance of the distress experienced by the individual seeking assistance, rather than then that of an illness state or the presumption of there being a problem. Distress is a more accurate description of how people feel.

MEMORANDUM OF AGREEMENT
An agreement mutually agreed by all sides that has been recorded as such. This is important because it gives both sides the safety net of having entered into a joint agreement that is understood as such. Of course such an agreement does not have to be set in stone and can be altered with the agreement of the partners involved.

OWNERSHIP
Again, self-explanatory, but important. The idea that you are the owner of your experience and own the process of your own recovery changes the basis of the normal power relationship between yourself and professionals.

PSYCHOSIS
Loaded with misunderstandings and anxiety. We do not think that psychosis is really any different from any other form of mental health difficulty.

RECOVERY (PROCESS)
The idea of recovery is both a goal and a process. We regard recovery to be the stage reached in your life where you have autonomy and freedom of action. There is never only one way to recover, each journey is different and has its own characteristics. It is helpful though to have a path to follow, even if you do not always stay on the path. It gives you some guidelines, a route that can sometimes save time and effort.

INTRODUCTION

Why a workbook?

This book has been written to fill a gap in the available literature on how to overcome mental distress. It has been written especially for people undergoing emotionally distressing experiences and particularly those people who have been diagnosed as having a mental illness. This is a WORKBOOK and as the name implies it is intended to be a practical tool in assisting you in your recovery. We are asking you to accept a personal challenge, one that you may find difficult and painful but one that offers the potential for personal change and discovery and a route to your own recovery. We intend this to be a positive and constructive experience. Why is the workbook needed?

Too often it is the case that the objectives of services intervening in the lives of people who are having mental health problems are necessarily limited to "maintenance", this is because there are not the resources or the staff time to do much more than this. The public image of mental health services and people with mental health problems is influenced by this situation. There is an impression that services for the mentally ill are only able to do the minimum. Therefore, it seems to many people that not much more can be achieved then to provide support to the individual by attempting to suppress the suffering, mainly through the administration of medication. There is very little time to help the person to heal, to recover from their illness and to live an autonomous and fulfilled life, this either seems to happen by itself or not at all. There is also another problem, and that is one of expectation, in some sectors of psychiatry if someone does "recover" it some how doesn't seem to fit into the traditional understanding of mental illness. The recovered person is likely to be regarded to be in "remission" (that is a temporary falling back of the disease process that will probably return) or as being wrongly diagnosed in the first place. On the other hand in the recent past even the term recovery has been co-opted by certain sectors of the mental health and psychiatric world. For them recovery is mainly the absence or reduction of symptoms that has been achieved through the administration of medication - we are recovered as long as we continue to take the medication - so for some maintenance is the same as recovery. This perspective of course neglects the important issue of the impact on an individuals quality of life that arise from being on long term medication, although the argument they would use is that this is better than the alternative, which is a return of the symptoms themselves.

The process of recovery remains some how mysterious and individual, seemingly not the central concern of the helping professions and not something that can be learned from. Fortunately, this is not always the case; many people recover from their mental distress, although their stories are mostly unknown. Many who recover have been assisted in their recovery by the involvement of committed and perceptive mental health workers. The reason that this has not become wide spread practice, is that for too long psychiatry has regarded mental illnesses and particularly what are known as serious mental illnesses, (like psychotic illnesses as evidence of a problem within the brain), as disease states. As a result there has not been much encouragement for this kind of work. Having put a clinical spin on mental distress, right from the beginning has had the unintended and unfortunate effect of alienating people from their own experiences. Our experiences, be they voices, wild delusions, anguish, fear, depression, have been integrated into the "disease", our narrative, our story becomes largely irrelevant, we stop being subject and become object. No wonder then that few professionals have shown much interest in our experiences, except as markers for a disease, they neither have the time nor the encouragement. Whilst this has surely increased misery and isolation, the services until recently rarely considered the importance of the life story of the person. Our experiences, beliefs, the circumstances of our lives and how we cope are not being harnessed to improve the quality of our lives.

Mapping recovery

In this new approach the important question then becomes what were the circumstances in which you had this experience and why did you feel so unable to cope with it. These are the building blocks of recovery (or healing) - it is a power taking process. Ownership of your experience is the first step, not to exalt in it, but to seek to understand the connections and the meanings. To do this you need the opportunity to talk about the experience itself and possibly to gain insight as a result, this is the route map we can use to extricate ourselves from difficult circumstances and to regain control of our lives again.

This is the goal of the workbook - we hope you find it inspiring and useful

WORKING TOGETHER

We believe that the most important factor in assisting people to begin the journey toward recovery is the value we place on the personal involvement of both the person with the mental health problem and the person who is designated as a mental health worker. To explain, we see each other as PEOPLE first, secondly as EQUAL PARTNERS in a defined process and thirdly as having different but MUTUALLY valuable expertise to offer. You are the EXPERT OF EXPERIENCE and the person you work with is an EXPERT BY PROFESSION. These are most important principles, it is only by turning them into a reality can we hope to work effectively together.

In this section we provide some advice and information that may be of assistance to you in developing a positive and constructive working relationship between you and the professional mental health worker (and of course the other way around), which are consistent with the principles above. They will also be useful in completing this workbook. It may be that you choose to complete the work book on your own or only involve a worker in some parts of the completion of the work book - that is up to you and is your right to decide to do what you think is best for you.

GOALS

We hope you find the following goals useful:

1. Redefining your experience

In this workbook our focus is on WELLNESS rather than illness. By shifting the focus from your mental health problems to your potential to recover means that the experiences that led you to use the mental health system in the first place can be thought of in a different light. This opens up the door to the possibility of a person centred approach (rather than an illness centred approach) where your experiences can be redefined outside of the usual reference points of psychiatry. We would encourage both you and your professional ally to consider first what your needs are and how they can be met, within the context of recovering your life and your autonomy.

2. Questioning

We hope this book will encourage you to ask questions about your treatment and how it is intended to assist you in your recovery. We hope it will give you the confidence to be assertive in your relationship with the services you use and to demand answers to the concerns that you have about your present situation and the future.

3. Starting with a clean sheet
Sometimes we can spend more time looking backwards than looking forwards, blaming ourselves' or others for things that went wrong in our lives. Although we can learn from our experiences it is also important to give ourselves permission to begin a new journey. That is why in this book we not only consider the past, but also focus on the future. What you want to do with your life is the important question, how you can achieve it is the most important task you face.

4. Why bother?
This book encourages you to take responsibility for the changes that you want to make in your life. Recovery demands from us a lot of hard work. We should not expect other people to do this for us.

5. Honesty
For many of us being honest about what we are experiencing has not always been a good idea and in some cases has led to negative reactions by workers and psychiatric services, who have responded by increasing our medication or requiring us to stay in hospital. This discourages people to be honest about sharing experiences and feelings

6. Making time
If you decide to embark on this journey of recovery it will need you to commit time and energy to give yourself the greatest chance of success.

Ground rules for working together
It is important if you are going to commence work on this enterprise and most especially if you are going to share this work with another person that you agree some basic ground rules. We propose the following:

The person who owns the experience owns this workbook
If it is decided that a paid person or friend is made aware of its contents then they do so in the knowledge that they accept these ground rules you need to develop your own ways of coping with your experiences. Any support you receive should reflect your own experience and definitions, not the person who is supporting you.

The experience is real
Trust should be earned; it cannot be taken for granted. We are all capable of, and have in the past broken trust - it is part of being human. Every time we ask for trust or give it, we give of ourselves, but on the other hand if we break that trust we lose part of ourselves. It is not a problem if the new coping strategies take time to work. There are many different ways of overcoming your problems and what works for one may not work for another. Do not be disheartened, progress is possible and even a partial success is better then not having tried at all.
Ownership
The workbook remains the property of the person who is using it. It is a personal record and if shared with another person this confidentiality should be respected. If you are a professional or friend, or simply giving this work book to someone to offer an alternative. If they choose to use it with you then you can use it as the common ground, where you both can meet,
and can identify what support they want from you to enable their own recovery.

Developing an action plan
Many professionals are required to plan and record what they do for us. We can use this to help our working relationship with the professionals. This plan should be focused around your experiences and how you understand them, and should work to your goals. The basis of most plans is some form of appraisal. There is no reason why this should not focus around you and your experiences. There is a guide at the end of this book for you and your chosen supporter to use for the work done in this book, as a base to identify your own plan of action.

An important message
We cannot and do not stress enough in this book that this work is ongoing and hard and at first you may not find the coping strategies immediately working.

It's OK when things don't work!!
They will in the long run, if not directly, by giving energy to looking at the ways you see your mental health problem and how you understand it. From this position you can try new ways and think of your own methods that will enable you to move from victim to victor.

We are always pleased to hear from people who have used this workbook and there is an evaluation form at the back for this purpose. If you can find time to give us your comments and experiences it can help us to improve this book and to develop further ones.

Developing A Strategy for Recovering from Mental Health problems
All mental health problems are in their own ways forms of survival strategies. One of the main concerns of this book is that the distress experienced, has an origin in life history and often relates to an unlivable situation. Uncovering the meaning of your experience is in its own way a further step to recovery.

On this topic our colleague and friend, Professor Marius Romme says:

"To be able to make the conceptual leap from the professional's theory to the patients experience, we need a new way of thinking about mental illnesses. In fact to think of 'reaction formations', and especially not to think in terms of specifically demarcated 'diseases', such as schizophrenia, manic-depressive psychosis and personality disorders like 'borderline'. Those labels are just part of a mindset which has no scientific validity. Such concepts have no basis in reality but are instead illusions or mental constructs made by the professional."

What Marius means by this is that mental illnesses are not diseases but rather complex reactions (or as he puts it reaction formations) to social situations and interactions. To be more precise, they have these features:

- They are reactions to problematic interactions with other people
- They are reactions to rules in society, which are difficult to accept for the individual
- They are an expression of the difficulty an individual may have with accepting the norms and values of certain groups in society

So, if the strange behaviors and experiences (also known as symptoms) are not the effect of some individualised but mysterious disease, but arise, somehow from your life experience then these experiences can become understandable and coherent. If you, as the person with these experiences are supported in understanding your 'illness' in the context of your life history. If the focus is you as a person rather than on the illness itself, then we can reach a new conclusion that it is the impact of the illness on your ability to cope with life that is both the issue and the solution.

This is why it is so important to enable the individual to triumph over their experiences. This can be achieved through accepting the experience as part of yourself (rather than an invasion of the self) and to gain insight into the meaning of your personal life. If this is accomplished, the difficult situation you can find yourself in will improve accordingly, the symptoms may disappear or you will find you can cope with them better.

Beginnings - working with professionals
Many people will have discussed assessments and other forms that they have to fill in with you. If you wish to own the process of recovery (which is a first step in the process of empowerment) you may want to place yourself at the beginning and the centre of the planning process. This is so that the plan that emerges will follow your expressed needs and wishes rather than focusing upon problems based on the views of other people, often formed without reference to you. To make the most of the resources that are available to help you, you need to make professionals work for you.

You need to be able to tell the person you want to work with some of your coping strategies and the way that you want them to work to support you on the road to recovery.

If you have completed the life history in this book you may wish to disclose elements of this to meetings of professionals reviewing your case. Write down before hand those things you feel it is important that people should know and also the conditions in which you wish them to be known i.e. that the information is confidential and should not be passed on without your consent.

Planning
You should, if possible, attend a planning meeting with someone you can trust, who is aware of what you want. Plan it before hand. If you don't wish to involve a friend or partner ask for the addresses of your local advocacy service. Write down what you want from services. There is no need to be specific. Take this with you to the meeting and be clear that the plan is for you, not to make life easier for the services. Be honest if you think it is important to have a job say so.

This workbook is necessarily limited in its scope. We know that there are other areas we should cover, but cannot in the space available. We hope you see that there is a process of emancipation that you can begin to enter and by using the principles of understanding your experience, organising and accepting them and by doing so starting to live your life again.

Good luck

PART ONE
WHAT RECOVERY MEANS TO ME
The Recovery Journey

" A journey of a thousand miles begins underneath your feet" (Chinese Proverb)

Recovery can be viewed as a personal journey and as such there are preparations that we can make to ensure that the journey is as comfortable as possible. Planning your journey is essential, a successful plan rarely happens by accident, though, sometimes, good fortune does play a part. The following are the stepping-stones of the recovery journey made by Ron Coleman one of the authors of this workbook.

The stepping-stones to recovery

First Stepping Stone:
Any recovery journey has a beginning, and for me the beginning was my meeting with support worker, it was her who encouraged me to go to the hearing voices self-help group in Manchester at the start of 1991. In a sense there were two elements at the beginning of my "Journey" these were my support worker and the self-help group.

Do you have a starting point or points for your journey?

If yes who or what are they?

Second Stepping Stone
There are other essentials required for a journey to be successful; one of these is the ability to be able to navigate to your desired destination. In this Ron was fortunate not to have one navigator but many. As Ron says; "These were people who kept me going in the right direction, through encouragement, friendship and guidance". Who are the people in your life that have given you encouragement, friendship or guidance and may be your navigators? "navigators require a map or a plan from which to navigate, and I have been fortunate in the people who were my own map- makers". An example of a map would be the personal recovery plan at the end of this book or your care plan.

Think of the mapmakers you identify with,. People therefore are one of the stepping-stones to recovery, take plenty of time to reflect on who your stepping-stones are or can be.
Identify who might be your navigators.

1)

2)

3)

4)

5)

(Continue this list if required)

We would like you to think about your most important relationships and describe what you feel about them.

1st relationship

How do you feel about this relationship?

2nd relationship

How do you feel about this relationship?

3rd relationship

How do you feel about this relationship?

4th relationship

How do you feel about this relationship?

5th relationship

How do you feel about this relationship?

The Second Stepping Stone

If I were to name all the people who have played a part in my recovery the list would be massive. The other thing about this list would be the fact that the majority on it would not be professionals. One of my fundamental beliefs about recovery is the premise that recovery cannot and does not happen in isolation. Nor can it happen if all our relationships are based around the professional and client interaction. Recovery is by definition wholeness and no one can be whole if they are isolated from the society, in which they live and work If people are the building bricks of recovery then the cornerstone must be self.

Self

"I believe without reservation that the biggest hurdle we face on our journey to recovery is ourselves. Recovery requires self-confidence, self-esteem, self-awareness and self-acceptance without this recovery is not just impossible, it is not worth it."

"For me these are the four selves; "
Self-confidence, Self- esteem , Self-awareness, Self-acceptance

These make up the second stepping-stone on the road to recovery.

What is your self-confidence like now?

What can you do to improve your self-confidence?

Set your self some tasks that will help you achieve the goals you have set above

Write about your level of self-esteem

Can you relate this to your mental health problem?

What can you do to improve your self-esteem?

Set some tasks that will help you increase your self-esteem

Take this opportunity to write about how self aware you are:

What can aid you in your pursuit of self-awareness?

How can you use this knowledge on your path to recovery?

Have you found self-acceptance?

If not can you write about the barriers you face in accepting your self

Develop some ways to breakdown these barriers

The Third Stepping Stone

"The third stepping stone is choice. You can choose to stop feeling sorry for your self and start living again, you can choose to stop being the poor little ill person and start the journey of recovery." In using this book you have made the choice to start your recovery, however you may have some fears about embarking on this journey.

What are your main fears about changing your life?

Fourth Stepping Stone

There is one other stepping stone in the recovery process and that is ownership. It is within ourselves that we will find the tools, strength and skills that we require to complete this journey, for it is within ourselves that the journey itself takes place.
What do you regard as being your main strengths?

PART TWO
ABOUT MYSELF

There is no doubt that our life history plays a large part in our mental health problems, most people in mental health services have had their life histories taken by professionals on more than one occasion. On the next few pages write your own story in your words emphasising the things that are important to you. For instance you might want to record the following kinds of life events:

The place I was born in

Some things I remember about my childhood

Some things I remember about school

Some things I remember about my adolescence

Important events in my adult life

When you are filling in this section you can either write a life story or you could record your life story on tape. Another way you could use is to think of your life as a river and draw the important events in your life along the river, alternatively you could draw a tree (roots for early childhood, the trunk representing your youth and the branches your adult life). Think creatively about how you record this information. If you want to use more pages then just add them to this section.

Your story

Your story (cont'd)

PART 3
MY NEEDS

"IN THE BEGINNING"
Every problem, illness, occurrence or event in our lives has to start somewhere. It is often the case that if we revisit the starting point of something that has happened, we find a means to deal with it. People in their every day lives often talk about the value of hindsight when reflecting on decisions they have made and how it would have changed their decisions. It therefore appears reasonable to us that when we are dealing with mental health problems that we should start at the beginning.

Use the rest of this page to write about your-self in the context of the beginning of your mental health problem. You can write about what was happening around you when the problem began, where you were, what you were doing, major events that happened around this time, how you were feeling when it all started and how services, family and friends responded to what was happening. You may even ask them to add their comments if you wish.

Now that you have written this up look at your response again and add anything you have missed out, then use the rest of this page to write how you might have changed things with the benefit of hindsight. You may also wish to write down how the services, your family and your friends might have responded differently towards your plight and what difference this response would have made to you.

Can you relate any parts of your life to your mental health problem? If so write these down exploring this relationship and ask yourself what can you do to help you resolve any issues?

Feelings play a large part in our mental well-being; it follows therefore that feelings play a large part in mental illness. It is important that you recognise your own feelings and the part they play in your personal mental health. It is also important that you recognise that these feeling are also a normal part of being a person. Below are a number of feelings, which you
may or may not have experienced in relation to your mental health problem. Circle those that apply to you and add in the space below any that are not listed.

Angry Fearless Sad Melancholy

Contented Anxious Powerless Despairing

Powerful Hopeless Isolated Afraid

Euphoric Mad Confused Worthless

Helpless Useless Love Resentful

Hatred Fear Terror Hope

Desire Hopeful fulfilled Anguish

Happy Surprise Fulfillment

Now that you have completed the above exercise you may like to take some time to reflect on the feelings you have circled. A useful thing to do at this point is to pick five of the most negative feelings and five of the most positive feelings and to explore how these feelings have impacted on your mental health.

1st Negative Feeling is:

The impact this feeling had on my mental health was/is:

2nd Negative Feeling is:

The impact this feeling had on my mental health was/is:

3rd Negative Feeling is:

The impact this feeling had on my mental health was/is:

4th Negative Feeling is:

The impact this feeling had on my mental health was/is:

5th Negative Feeling is:

The impact this feeling had on my mental health was/is:

1st Positive Feeling is:

The impact this feeling had on my mental health was/is:

2nd Positive Feeling is:

The impact this feeling had on my mental health was/is:

3rd Positive Feeling is:

The impact this feeling had on my mental health was/is:

4th Positive Feeling is:

The impact this feeling had on my mental health was/is:

5th Positive Feeling is:

The impact this feeling had on my mental health was/is:

Look through these feelings you have identified and in two paragraphs one for the positive and one for the negative write up how these feelings have changed since you first experienced them. For example you may have changed the way you cope with your feelings.

Positive Feelings

Negative Feelings

PART FOUR
My strengths

Understanding the impact that your feelings have had or still have on your mental health will help you develop coping strategies for those negative feelings that will allow you to own these feelings without them disabling you. Likewise understanding your positive feelings can allow you to have them without the guilt that sometimes you have when you dare to enjoy yourself.

Answer the following questions.

When was the last time you did something to please yourself, and then felt badly afterwards?

What was it you did?

What were the feelings that made you feel bad?

Why do you think you felt like this?

What do you think you can do so that you might feel differently in the future?

Plan something to enjoy in the near future, using what you have learned from before to try to avoid feeling bad.

What were the circumstances?

How did it make you feel?

If this situation arose again what would you want to happen?

PART FIVE
MY MENTAL HEALTH CAREER

Recovery is essentially a personal thing and as such is experienced differently by each individual. One common theme though is our ability to make choices in our lives. Another common theme is that we often have had to make use of mental health services. In this section we are concentrating on your experience of mental health services. Do you feel you have been offered choices in the past? If not why not? Can we change that for the better, so that you can have a better service in the future?

NB This section is also useful for workers. It is part of an exercise that involves identifying the kinds of support and assistance that you would value as well as sharing your experiences to date of the mental health system. The worker can gain more insight into your feelings and your life history including your relationship with mental health services. This is your chance to give some feed back and maybe get some explanations.

1. Choices and experience

What has been your experience of mental health services (has it been positive, negative or somewhere in between)?

What was your best experience?

What was your worst experience?

What was the experience you remember the most?

2. Choices and decisions

"Most people in our society regard choice as a fundamental human right and correctly so, indeed one can argue that the level of sophistication in society can be measured by the level of choice an individual can make within it". Choice is one of the central themes in mental health and is particularly important when it concerns issues that direct you like what treatment we are given or what other kinds of support we are identified as needing (like housing, employment, etc.).

Services do not always get this right, because they see our vulnerability first they often feel it is necessary to take decisions on our behalf.

Has this ever happened to you?

What were the circumstances?

How did it make you feel when it happened?

How do you feel about it now?

If this situation arose again what would you want to happen?

3. Choices and knowing what the options are
Sometimes the choices we are offered often seem cosmetic. Rarely are the choices offered really meaningful. All too often the notion of choice is quite limited and being offered choice basically means which drug treatment we take. This is sometimes happening because we are not considering the full range of options available.

Have you ever felt that you were not offered a real choice?

YES NO SOMETIMES

What were the circumstances?

How did it make you feel?

If this situation arose again what would you want to happen?

4. Choices: Asking questions and getting answers
Today, we have the NHS patients' charter and this clearly states that all alternatives should be discussed with you. The problem is that sometimes both you and mental health workers have few ideas about what alternatives are available, beyond the use of medication. We need to think about what other kinds of alternatives are available. This might mean that you, along with a worker could explore what sort of interventions and support are available in your area and to see if they would benefit you.

What treatment and care support do you receive now?

What treatments have you received in the past?

Have these treatments and other forms of support been helpful or not (explain which ones were helpful or not and explain why this is the case)?

Do you feel you were fully consulted and involved in the decisions reached about your treatment?

If not, why not and what happened?

5. Choosing the people who support you

One of the most important aspects of choice is in choosing the people who support you. The usual practice of appointing a key-worker to work with you without consultation is not only wrong but can in some circumstances can be an area of unnecessary conflict between you and the professional. How often have you and your key-worker been asked whether they you happy working together? If there is no positive relationship between you and the professional this can have a very negative impact on your recovery.

Services can allow you to choose your own support workers. The other identified benefit is that a trusting relationship is established much more quickly using this system thereby speeding the recovery process.

Ron says "Even if the system cannot adopt a method that allows the client to choose their paid supports it must at the very least find a way to allow the client to change their paid supports if they wish to do so. If this simple step could be achieved then it is my opinion that the benefit in terms of recovery will far outweigh any loss of face that may occur amongst professionals"

Do you have a good relationship with your key worker?
If, yes, why is it a good relationship, if not, why not?

PART SIX
MY MEDICATION (and other forms of treatment)

Medication plays a large part in treatments for many mental health problems. Medication can be useful in helping people to cope with distressing feelings, but sometimes they can also cause some problems. In this section we want you to think about your medication (if you take it) and how it affects your life. If you are not sure about the answers to these questions it might be helpful to ask for the assistance of your key worker (or you could ask the hospital pharmacist or your psychiatrist).

What medication are you taking at this time? (include all your medicines from your psychiatrist and your GP for mental and physical health problems).

1) 2) 3)

4) 5) 6)

How does these medications effect you?

Positive ones

1)

2)

3)

4)

5)

6)

Negative ones

1)

2)

3)

4)

5)

If your medication has been changed, what other medications have you taken in the past?

1) 2)

How did these medication(s) affect you?

Positive

Negative

Why was the medication changed?

What is the amount of medication that you take daily (indicate the quantity for different medicines if taking more than one)?

Has the amount of medication you take been changed?

More

Less

Why?

How do you take the medication? For instance do you take the medication as it is prescribed or only when you feel you need it?

Tablets Injections Other

Do you think you are able to decide for yourself about the medicines you take and when you take them? If not why not?

what other treatment do you get or have been given in the past , for instance psychotherapy, psychology, electro-convulsive Therapy, counseling, CBT, group work, stress/anxiety management, other?

How did the treatment affect you?

Positive

Negative

Are there medications or other treatments that you want to try?

If you do, what are they?

Why?

Have you had any complementary treatments (acupuncture, aromatherapy, massage, herbal medicine and homeopathy etc.). If you have what are they?

What has been the effect?

Positive

Negative

Are there others that you would like to try?
What are they?

Why?

PART SEVEN

PLANS FOR CHANGE

The ability to make choices in services now rests on how well the care programme approach (CPA) or case management approach (CMA) is working in your area. These are the two assessment tools that are now used to identify what professionals think the client needs and also what the client's aspirations are. This could provide an opportunity to plan your recovery journey.

Have you had an assessment under the Care Programme Approach or Care Management Approach?

YES
NO

If you have, what does it say (you could stick it in here or summarise it)?

Are you satisfied with your CPA/CMA, if you are, why? If not, why not?

What do you think your CPA/CMA would say if it was more focused on your recovery?

Starting today, what kinds of assistance would you like to have, even if they are not available at this time (this is like a wish list)?

Ron recalls "When I saw the consultant during the ward round, I always had lots of questions and came out with no answers. The main reason I never got any answers was that I always forgot the questions in the heat of the meeting. This problem was eventually resolved when I finally agreed with my advocate to write down my questions before I saw the consultant. When they came round. Though most of my questions still went unanswered I at least had the satisfaction of knowing I had asked them"

What questions would you like to ask your psychiatrist?

What questions would you like to ask your key worker?

PART EIGHT
YOUR PERSONAL DEVELOPMENT PLAN

Planning your future

Making a good plan could enable you to plot your own journey to recovery and ensure that you stay on course during the journey. There are many ways of planning that can be used that are person centred.

Ron says; "The one that I prefer is a personal development plan much like the ones that most professionals use in their own workplaces. The reason for my preference is that the focus of this type of plan is very much on development rather than on care. This does not mean that we reject the concept of care indeed in my opinion working in this way can only enhance the quality of care provided by adding the notion of 'caring about' to the existing 'caring for' framework. Like most planning the personal development plan requires the person to answer a series of questions".

The following are a selection the types of questions that we think it would be useful to include in these plans:

What areas of your life do you consider have gone particularly well over the last six months?

What you or other people to build on your success could do?

What areas of your life have not gone so well in the last six months?
Have there been any particular barriers, difficulties or problems that have caused these parts of your life not to go so well?

What can you do by yourself to resolve these problems?

What can others do to help you resolve these problems?

What do you want to achieve over the next six months?

Which of these goals can you achieve on your own?

Which of these goals do you require help to achieve?

Who can help you achieve these goals?

All of the above questions may appear straight forward, but when was the last time we were asked them by others, or indeed asked our-selves, any of them. These questions are fairly open-ended in that they can relate to health, social activities, employment or training. They also allow you to look at your strengths, weaknesses, opportunities and threats (SWOT) in your personal life. This SWOT analysis can if used properly by all concerned lead the recovery process by allowing you to monitor your own progress against the goals you have set yourself.

PART NINE
MY PRIORITIES

This stage involves looking back at everything you have written and to decide upon the most important things you need to change, in order to work toward your recovery. It will probably help you at this stage if you work with someone who knows you well, as this can be the most difficult part to complete. Include difficulties that you want to overcome, but also the positive things you want to develop. We want you to do this just for the next three months, six and nine months.

Things about my life I would like to change in the next THREE months

What I would like to be the outcome of this change

Steps I need to take to make this change

People I would like to help me

Barriers to achieving this change

Repeat this process for each change you want to make.
Remember to review your progress and record how much you have achieved in fulfilling your goals.

Things about my life I would like to change in the next SIX months

What I would like to be the outcome of this change

Steps I need to take to make this change

People I would like to help me

Barriers to achieving this change

Repeat this process for each change you want to make.
Remember to review your progress and record how much you have achieved in fulfilling your goals.

Things about my life I would like to change in the next NINE months

What I would like to be the outcome of this change

Steps I need to take to make this change

People I would like to help me

Barriers to achieving this change

Repeat this process for each change you want to make. Remember to review your progress and record how much you have achieved in fulfilling your goals.

The A - Z to coping with mental health problems

Accept the reality of your experience
Break through the victim barrier
Consider all your options
Develop coping strategies that suit you
Enter a real alliance with a professional or friend
Focus on your experience
Go into a self-help group (if there is one)
Help others by sharing your experience (you are an expert of experience)
Identify the areas of your life that you need to work on
Join in activities outside of mental health organisations
Keep a diary
Live your life not your label
Make space for yourself
Negotiate for what you want
Own your experience
Perseverance is the name of the game
Question your treatment and diagnosis
Reward yourself when you succeed
Small is beautiful
Take your time, haste can mean failure
Use services to your advantage
Victories are to fought for
Work on your weaknesses
Xperiment with different coping strategies
You make your decisions, not other people
Zap your negative feelings by taking control of them

Memorandum of Agreement

Coping strategies can only be understood by understanding the belief system of the individual experiencing mental distress, this is something that professionals can find hard to accept. This is not a personal failing but rather a product of their training. So can we work through our experience to a successful resolution without the involvement of professionals especially if they refuse to work within our frames of reference? The answer is yes, but it does make it much harder as we will always be in conflict about the way forward.

It is therefore in both parties interest to negotiate a way of working together that may require compromise on both sides. If this can be achieved it can become the basis of a meaningful working relationship.

We think it is useful to write out the nature of the agreement between yourself and the professional you are working with. So, fill in the space below with the specific points you have agreed and then date and sign it. (Points you might include how often and when you will meet; confidentiality issues; a statement about honesty; the nature of the services provided etc.

The following statement is an agreement made between ___________________
(name) and _____________________(name)

This agreement determines how we shall work together.

Signed

Signed

Remember that you are at the centre of this process, it is there to support not disable you. You have the right to expect a good quality service.

Treatment wishes of_______________________

To whom it may concern I____________________ being of sound mind on this date ________

I would like to record that in the event of me being treated without my informed consent would like the following to be considered and adhered to as is my expectation of your respect for my human rights.

I do not want the following treatments to be given to me

Please list (for instance some people list ECT, certain medications etc.)

I would like the following approaches to be considered as a priority and my wishes (for instance a people list, leave me alone, let me lie in bed, listen when I speak with you, listen to my experiences, maintain my respect and dignity as a person)

Please contact the following people in the event of my admission to hospital and whom I would like to be involved as my representative.

Name

Address

Telephone

Please note that the following person is to be regarded as my representative above my legally defined next of kin.

Name

Address

Telephone

The solicitor authorised to act on my behalf in matters concerning my mental health and liberty is:

Name

Address

Telephone

(If desired)

To my key worker___________________________

Please record this information in my case notes/care plans/records. As my paid professional support I expect you to act with the utmost consideration of my interests.

I__________________ (key worker) recognise the wishes of ______________ and agree that I will always endeavor to act in the interests of _______________ and to make people aware of these choices in treatment pathways.

In this book, the third in a series of workbooks for recovery we look at the lessons that we have been learning about the recovery process. We have turned these into a practical guide, so that any one who wants to take this journey can benefit from Ron' s experience and the many other people we have talked to about their own recoveries. This book is not intended to be the answer, it is instead a tool for your own recovery journey.

Paul Baker March 2000

Published by P&P Press